THE WORLDS OF ARCHITECTURAL DIGEST

NEW YORK INTERIORS

THE WORLDS OF ARCHITECTURAL DIGEST

NEW YORK INTERIORS

EDITED BY PAIGE RENSE

EDITOR-IN-CHIEF, ARCHITECTURAL DIGEST

THE KNAPP PRESS   PUBLISHERS   LOS ANGELES

THE VIKING PRESS   DISTRIBUTORS   NEW YORK

Published in the United States of America in 1979
The Knapp Press
5900 Wilshire Boulevard, Los Angeles, California 90036
Copyright © 1979 by Knapp Communications Corporation
All rights reserved
First Edition

Distributed by The Viking Press
625 Madison Avenue, New York, New York 10022

Distributed simultaneously in Canada by Penguin Books Canada Limited

Library of Congress Cataloging in Publication Data
Main entry under title: New York interiors.
(The Worlds of Architectural digest)
Selections from the pages of Architectural digest, newly edited and designed.
1. Interior decoration—New York (City) I. Rense, Paige.
II. Architectural digest. III. Series.
NK2002.N48   1979   747'.8'83097471   79-84686

ISBN 0-89535-031-9
Printed and bound in the United States of America

CONTENTS

FOREWORD

There seems to be little middle ground when it comes to discussing New York City—or, more accurately, Manhattan. For many people it is a city filled with vibrancy and magic; for others it is a nightmare of inconvenience and manic confusion. Nonetheless, there is no great city in the world quite like it. Paris has feminine charms and London masculine elegance, but New York has its own unique and electric identity. Those of you who are familiar with the city, however, will no doubt agree with me that its magic and electric aureole is precisely what makes it such a difficult place in which to live. In fact, I feel that there are few other cities in the world where the personal home environment is of such overriding importance. Somehow—in the interests of sanity and identity and freedom of the spirit—the crowds and concrete and skyscrapers, the frenzy of taxicabs and buses and subways must be held at bay. A home here must indeed be a castle, if not a fortress.

For these reasons I am confident that you will perceive, as you turn the following pages, why the New York home or apartment is of such significance in the field of interior design. The challenge to the individual designer is immense, for he or she must create, whether on a small or a large scale, what is essentially a retreat from the urban landscape. As you will see, that retreat can take many forms, and I have selected for this particular volume adapted and revised samples of the best New York design that has appeared in the pages of ARCHITECTURAL DIGEST over the years.

The solutions to the problem of creating a viable and comfortable and personal environment in what is basically an impersonal if not, indeed, a cruel city are many. It is no secret that New York is the most European of cities in the United States, and treasures from all parts of the world arrive in its great port daily. Thus the tastes of interior designers and homeowners alike are intriguingly varied. Here you will find almost everything: pure eighteenth-century décor, both European and American, and styles ranging from the most classical to the most starkly contemporary, from the intricacies of Art Nouveau to the severity of the Bauhaus. There are penthouses overlooking Central Park and SoHo lofts and one-room studios, Sutton Place townhouses and Fifth Avenue apartments. On the surface they appear to have very little in common, but it seems to me that closer inspection reveals the theme of unity I have mentioned: the desire to create a small warm world within the context of a larger and colder one. Design in New York is that simple, and that complicated.

It has never been my desire to tell you that one interior design is better than another but only to show, without comment, the décor that seems to me most typical and most enduring. In this effort I have had a good deal of help. I owe gratitude, not only to my editors and photographers and writers, but to innumerable interior designers and patient homeowners. And, above all, I owe gratitude to the many loyal and concerned readers of ARCHITECTURAL DIGEST.

Paige Rense
Editor-in-Chief
Los Angeles, California

THE WORLDS OF ARCHITECTURAL DIGEST

NEW YORK INTERIORS

IN THE CLASSIC MODE

No other period styles are so often revived and copied for interiors as those of eighteenth-century France and England. Yet it is astounding how little of the original wit and inventive spirit emerges in the countless imitations. For over a century, American interior design has dedicated itself to grafting republican, if not Puritan, principles onto the eighteenth century's clearly aristocratic modes and styles. This results in elegant designs of an earlier age locked into overly constrained roles by the tedious conformity of so-called good taste.

Fortunately, this is not the path taken by New York City interior designer George Clarkson. He is a past master at creating interiors that bring back all the ebullience and vitality of the classic eighteenth-century vocabulary. This Park Avenue duplex, which he designed with a remarkably rich selection of the furnishings of the Age of Elegance, comes joyously alive in what can only be described as a very grand setting. But it is a setting whose animation and charm make it a perfect environment for its inhabitants, whom Mr. Clarkson simply describes as "a very proper couple with two beautiful children."

Clearly, the designer is as intuitive about the living potential of his clients as he is knowledgeable about every detail of period style. He is blessed as well with a brilliant sense of color. These qualities allow him maximum agility in handling design situations and details that to many would seem impossible. He is, in fact, one of those rare designers who never complains about the "problems" involved in a new design. That catalogue of agonies in the standard design saga is swept aside by his clear-eyed professionalism. "But," he cautions, "you can't just say you're going to do something and go tack it all up randomly. You need a good firm foundation, or it's really not going to work at all."

Here everything works. The apartment is happily devoid of all the obvious but misguided decorative excesses of floral fever or off-white understatement to which eighteenth-century furnishings adamantly refuse to submit with grace. "I think it's difficult to have a majestic room, an important room, and just have it full of flowers. And certainly in this case," Mr. Clarkson adds, speaking of the Louis XV boiserie-paneled salon, "the room wouldn't sit well with anything like the 'bowers of flowers' approach." The magic, he feels, had to come from the contrast of a very French room filled with English furniture. A magnificent antique Oushak in dominant tones of salmon, beige and mauve was chosen to provide much-needed unity. The boiseries were washed in a mauve that echoes the carpet, and the ceiling is sponged with the same color to give a light suggestion of clouds. Draperies and sofa were done in what the designer calls "the most elegant cotton thing I could imagine." The soft outlines of the warp print, the robust design and the drenching colors anchor the overall coordination and vitality of the room's background. Against this he has contrasted objects and pieces of furniture that "purposely don't harmonize but give depth and feeling."

In a similar way, he has adroitly balanced moods between rooms throughout the entire apartment. Although casually dismissing his stylistic tour de force by saying he let "the architecture control what we did," he has kept the visual pace brisk. The apartment is a controlled orchestration of diverse and splendid elements, and George Clarkson's sure hand can be seen in the luxuriant details and the challenging interplay of colors. Nonchalantly, he says that things are what they are because a room "can handle them," modestly ignoring his own great fund of imagination and culture.

Designer George Clarkson created this elegant New York City apartment. PRECEDING PAGE: *French paneled doors open to reveal the classically austere Entrance Hall. A graceful statue of Bacchus is framed by the curves of the staircase.* ABOVE AND OPPOSITE ABOVE: *An Oushak rug softly underscores the warm shades of the traditionally appointed Living Room. French boiserie contrasts with 18th-century English furnishings.*

OPPOSITE BELOW: *A lacquer Louis XV console displays a delicate floral arrangement, paired 18th-century bronze-doré elephants and an alert Meissen spaniel. A Directoire landscape-papered screen provides a scenic backdrop.* LEFT: *The bright tones of the Dining Room walls set off the deep-hued polished wood of airy Chippendale chairs. Door and window detailing in the style of Adam amplifies the room's classical mode.*

BELOW AND RIGHT: *A 19th-century painted bed becomes an architectural element in a delicately precise Bedroom. The bed's artfully draped and shirred canopy creates a classical dome, counterpointing gingham upholstery and the pale geometrics of the durrie carpeting.*

14

CONTEMPORARY ACCENT

It is a rare occasion when an interior designer admits that a recently completed project is "the culmination of many years of work." But Jay Spectre is entirely convincing when he speaks of an apartment he designed, high above Fifth Avenue in Manhattan. "You see, it is the softening of a point of view," he says in calm southern tones. "It is what it is, with emphasis on comfort and elegance."

A first glance at these polished rooms yields an impression of traditionalism, of modern objects and paintings being worked delicately into an overall aesthetic. But a closer consideration of the apartment quickly offers evidence to the contrary. Mr. Spectre is firmly of the 1970s in his use of scale and proportion. He catches the essence, the integrity of an age in a few carefully observed details—rather like a telling sketch dashed off by a master draftsman.

Having decided to avoid major structural alterations—which are often futile anyway, according to Mr. Spectre, who believes that modern buildings present "unchangeable and awkward architectural conditions"—he chose to explore the possibility of beguilement with the use of light and mirrors. The terrace that jutted abruptly into the living room was softened by being lined with solar bronze glass. With a Maillol sculpture and two ficus trees placed on the terrace, easing the transition, it became an integral part of the visual experience of the room.

Mr. Spectre has a happy way of exploding preconceived notions: "Low ceilings? I enjoy dealing with them," he states. "They are a fact of modern life, and we might as well make the most of them. After all, few people have rooms that can properly accommodate extremely tall furniture."

Working with such proportions has led the designer to reconsider his usual vertical style: "There is a markedly horizontal emphasis in this apart-ment," he explains. "I kept all the elements low, in order to create a sense of depth and space. This formed a sort of deep focus, an illusion of distance—factors that are necessary when viewing paintings and sculpture. Working with art is a privilege, and so is the experience of collaborating with a client who has an eye for fine things."

Lighting can also mold the atmosphere, and Mr. Spectre takes great pains over it: "Light troughs of my own design are used throughout," he points out. "In the living room they're of brushed steel, while in the hall polished bronze is employed to wash the walls and the art with warm, clear light."

Everywhere in the apartment the glow of fine polished surfaces is evident. Jay Spectre is one of a handful of contemporary designers who have the ability to use the most luxurious materials without creating effects that are claustrophobic or crassly sumptuous. The ultimate goal of all complex work is to appear simple—even artless. But, as all those who have fallen under the spell of such perfection know, quality is the first resort of sophistication.

"In retrospect, when I think of my career," says the designer, "I realize that there is a certain truth to the old cliché about only being as good as your client. In this case it was a lady of unusual taste, who genuinely wanted a creative person to work with her. And she appreciated professionalism, which, surprisingly, frightens many people. Having a rapport like that gives an indefinable tang to the work—a certain relaxed quality."

Characteristically, the designer has made his work appear far simpler than it really is. And this is the real mark of talent: the ability to make the final result seem easy and entirely obvious. It is a talent that Jay Spectre possesses in full measure and uses to perfection in this New York apartment.

OPPOSITE: *Another view of the Living Room takes in a Maillol Venus on the greenery-lined terrace. Etchings by Rembrandt are included in a wall gallery, below which a Hugo Robus sculpture,* Woman Washing Her Hair, *forms a graceful arch.* RIGHT: *The stainless-steel-and-mirror-edged window overlooks a view of Central Park South.*

PRECEDING PAGES: *The Entrance Hall is also a gallery where a Henry Moore reclining-woman sculpture establishes rocklike centrality. The sweeping shapes of a Frankenthaler painting and an Avery interior scene complement the earthy form of a pre-Columbian figure.*

OPPOSITE: *Maillol's* Torse de Vénus *is a serene presence on the brick-floored garden Terrace. Delicately patterned Chinese jardinières hold leafy greenery. In the distance, the hazy evening sky and brilliantly sparkling lights of Manhattan are reminders of the bustling world outside.*

ABOVE: *In the Dining Room, curving chairbacks of mellow wood establish a rhythmic line. Spectre-designed lighting troughs add a sleek contemporary element to the room, emphasizing the glow of an animated 18th-century Japanese screen. Brass vitrines hold a collection of antique Chinese pieces; versatile parchment-topped steel dining tables can function as single units or in combination for evenings of entertaining.*

THE GLAMOUR OF THE ECLECTIC

"Glamorous and eclectic with three terraces" is one friend's way of describing Lionel Larner's garden-surrounded New York penthouse. Mr. Larner, a theatrical agent, is rather more relaxed, describing it as "a place to live quietly on those few occasions when I do have time to myself."

Running a personal service agency for a roster of stars that includes such names as Glenda Jackson, Carroll O'Connor, Anne Baxter, Diana Rigg and David McCallum leaves Lionel Larner with a particularly crowded engagement schedule. He lives in a world where everything has to be juggled: conferences, openings, dinners. "I have no regular schedule for relaxation," he comments, "and I wanted a quiet 'retreat' in mid-Manhattan."

The penthouse's garden-sized terrace does make it seem as if it were "a little house in the country." In summer, the open, sun-filled interiors become pavilions extending and joining the roof gardens, and the living room is transformed into a very grand antechamber to the front terrace. Here Mr. Larner virtually lives in fine weather: breakfasting with friends, having summer dinner parties or just spending a day reading scripts. This favorite area's rather European formality suits him perfectly.

In winter, however, the art-filled rooms come into their own, and, awash with light from the high undraped windows, they maintain their pervasive garden atmosphere. White walls, some large plants, bare oak floors and white slipcovers on invitingly plump upholstered furniture reinforce the country mood; and a constantly crackling living room fire sets a tone of warmth and worldly well-being. Even the most unobservant eye sees at first glance that this is no ordinary room. The décor, reflecting the mood, is thoughtful, polished, elegant, yet disarmingly informal. One touch of Lionel Larner's style is exemplified by a tall stack of picture books supporting a Giacometti plaster lamp at one end of the sofa. "Things are either really functional or in bad taste," he says. "My books are beautiful, and I love them near me. I didn't have a table that was high enough to hold the lamp. So what could be nicer than a pile of books under it? It was practical."

His extraordinary and distinctive collection of art ambles freely from Matisse to Léger to Orozco to Pascin and van Dongen, and on to Marsden Hartley, Sam Francis and David Hockney. "One must buy things one loves," he states. "Things end up where they're required, although at the same time I have definite ideas of what form and line should be like. I put the large pictures on the bottom and the small ones on top. This is an evolution, not a 'decorated' apartment—just a small place that expands and evolves somewhat by trial and error."

The easy elegance and personal charm of Lionel Larner's penthouse come not at all from advanced refinements of contemporary design or from any overall design theory, but from the vitality of the owner, and from a very personal selection of objects both well loved and well used. He is very clear about the various requisites he had in mind for his home. As the background for a busy theatrical agent's life, a life devoted in every sense to entertainment, the penthouse functions as a flexible setting for the many parties he gives. But there are, he feels, more important elements. "Quality is the great priority. There has to be personal response and quality about everything in my life—from a new client to a new object. Somehow they have to speak to me. I have no interest in the 'exquisite lifestyle in the sky' sort of apartment. That isn't me at all. What I do respond to are people and books and their style, to art and interiors and *their* style."

OPPOSITE: *Light from a sunny outdoor terrace floods the studiolike Living Room. Slipcovered furnishings maintain an informal feeling; a book-framed doorway repeats the shape of the mirror-edged fireplace. Resting on a table near* Bather, *a large sculpture by Bernard Reder, are a Ch'ien Lung bowl and an African ivory antelope.* RIGHT: *Seen from another angle, Reder's* Bather *basks in the glow of a classic Giacometti lamp casually placed atop a stack of books.*

A sectioned 17th-century Italian landscape forms a mysterious, dark panorama against the light-washed walls of the Living Room. A Louis XVI console holds K'ang Hsi famille noire porcelain vases, a de Creeft sculpture and a Giacometti lamp. Works by Matisse brighten the wall above. More art grouped around the doorway includes paintings by Kuhn, Bischoff and Bisttran.

The softly lit Dining Room is enhanced by a wall of shelves that hold an extensive collection of Ming and Ch'ing blue-and-white porcelains. The elegant heirloom table setting and sprightly patterned cloth sparkle invitingly in an effective contrast to the generally muted tones of the room.

LEFT: *In the Master Bedroom, carefully juxtaposed artworks by Van Dongen, Hartley, Picasso and Pascin surround a trunk used as a base for a Pevsner sculpture. A shaped Okimoto canvas hangs above an 18th-century Spanish portrait; beneath a console, an Allen Jones lithograph whimsically extends a foot.*

LEFT: *Curvilinear Belle Epoque chairs and a French garden table grace the outdoor Terrace. The peaceful atmosphere is enlivened by masses of greenery and an Italian allegorical figure; the metropolitan view lies beyond.*

THE APPEAL OF SIMPLICITY

Stepping across the threshold is like entering another life. All is calm and ordered. The walls are a liberating white. The spaces, composed with infinite care, unfold silently in several different directions, like an opening fan. Here the sounds of Manhattan are as inconsequential as the distant boom of the sea might be. Interior designer David Whitcomb's apartment seems almost an island adrift in time. He is, of course, levelheaded in the way all magicians and creators of private worlds must be.

"Designers are prone to feel that they have to walk into a space and change it drastically," he says. "On the other hand, I am perfectly willing to modify an apartment, to create my particular universe through the gentle art of assemblage. So what you see around you that is in any way structural — the 'container,' if you will — is the work of John Saladino, whose apartment this was before I bought it. I feel that I was able to retain the spirit of his structure and to echo its quality. I repeated his device of the mirrored living room ceiling in my bedroom, because I admired the tremendous sense of expansion it gave the space. At the same time, I took things I already owned and placed them in such a way as to convert the apartment completely into my own personal statement — without, I hope, blurring the integrity of the original."

Indeed, there is much that is fascinating about David Whitcomb's creation. Above all, there is that lively sense of the fertile eye, as the French call it. "Yes," says Mr. Whitcomb, "I think the harmonies are there. A certain relationship in terms of size and color will link together pieces from many different eras. And I've always been fascinated by the continuing beauty of ancient objects."

Despite the opulence of individual objects, the final effect of the apartment is one of spareness and selectivity. "Surely it's logical to live simply nowadays," says the designer. "A while back I walked into an apartment I'd done several years ago, and I thought, 'Good Lord, it's so very heavy.' We really are entering a period of great purity of design now. To take only one example, look at the way lamps have begun to disappear from interiors. The fact is nobody wants a Chinese vase with a shade perched on top anymore. A lighting system that fits clearly and succinctly into the functional scheme of things makes so much more sense."

How does designing a personal space differ from working for a client? "Well, of course, it all becomes terribly introspective. I discover my own growth each time I move. It's an awareness that becomes more brilliantly highlighted each time. You find yourself really examining your needs. Then this new self-knowledge gets applied to commissions. This is a personal point of view, I know, but the rooms that really fascinate me are almost always not designed at all, at least in the usual way. I like to imagine that an apartment or a house constitutes a visual biography of the person involved. I don't feel that a room should ever be set up to form a static situation. Certainly everything changes — human beings, most of all. Be rigorous, be intellectual — but allow the emotions to shine through."

It has often been said that art in the final analysis comes down to feeling, and the intrinsic value of David Whitcomb's design for himself is based upon just such a refinement. It is all here: the loving appreciation of fine furniture expertly placed, the evenness of the flow of space from room to room, the effortless balancing of objects, the subtle acknowledgment of the past. To the designer's mind, it is very simple indeed: "Personality should dictate all the uses of space."

An aura of conscious order pervades the Manhattan apartment of designer David Whitcomb. PRECEDING PAGE: *Antique objets d'art—including a 1st-century Roman urn and a Chinese porcelain dog—acquire new importance within the austerity of the Living Room.*

BELOW: *The light-toned quilted sofa and stools, vertical blinds and bleached oak flooring establish a linear motif in the living room. Springlike bouquets, a brass Berrocal sculpture placed on a Charles X table, and a serpent-entwined English Mithraic figure add visual fillips.*

BELOW: *A classically ornamented Régence commode exemplifies the designer's use of 18th-century decorative objects. Hiding behind the leaves of a plant is a tiny pottery lion.*

BELOW: *A mirrored ceiling reflects the transition from living room to Dining Room, guarded by a Japanese terra-cotta wrestler. The rich carpeting, recessed lighting and striped walls provide a sleek background for the custom-designed table flanked by a banquette and 18th-century English footed chairs.*

BELOW: *An imposing abstract painting by contemporary artist Claudio Bravo fills a wall in the Hallway. A tall and graceful lacquer stand topped by an Egypto-Roman pegmatite urn dating from the 1st century distinguishes the raised and carpeted entrance to the bedroom.*

OPPOSITE: *In the Bedroom, architectural elements blend with antiques, such as the Regency amphora and a Chinese porcelain bottle. An 18th-century English painting,* Four Musicians, *strikes a lively note.*

AN IMPRESSIONISTIC LOOK

New York interior designer Mario Buatta exudes a special kind of warmth and friendliness on first meeting that might take others years to establish. Those who know him well are forever recounting charming anecdotes about how he will show up for a weekend in the country carrying boxes of Italian pastries or send packets of chili through the mail with hand-drawn notes. It is this childlike imagination and sense of humor, mixed with a highly styled sense of taste, that has made his name a household word in some extraordinary households.

In the context of his own apartment on the East Side of Manhattan, however, Mr. Buatta presents an entirely different image. "I am a collector," he states emphatically. "I suppose most designers are. I love a house that is full of things that have been collected for years, and I love having what you call clutter around me—organized clutter, that is. I really can't bear parting with things, since so many of them tell a story important to me. Maybe it is difficult for anyone to understand what I'm trying to accomplish here. There certainly is a lot to see!"

And indeed there is: a splendid lacquered Queen Anne secretary cabinet, circa 1720, with a double-bonnet top; ripe, round cabbages and delicate asparagus stalks of porcelain that form unusual still lifes on skirted tables; oval Chinese mirror paintings lovingly sashed and bowed with faille; double-gourd Oriental vases perched atop eighteenth-century Adam brackets; small bookcases crammed with Cecil Beaton diaries, gardening books and a few scattered fabric and wallpaper samples.

The living room is a charming mixture, suggesting a bit of Hogarth and a good deal of Regency, with the overall feeling of an English country house. Nothing, however, is quite as haphazard as it appears, and Mr. Buatta has provided the room with a certain symmetry. "It's all in the balance, you see," he explains. "Often I decorate a room the way you might paint a picture. I like my colors clear and fresh, almost like an Impressionist or a Hans Hofmann painting. And I like to be daring enough to use colors that, at first glance, look as if they won't work. I am very fond of blue and white and yellow, and I manage to use a good deal of these colors in most of my work."

John Fowler, the legendary English decorator, had a significant and most profound effect on Mr. Buatta's design philosophy and sense of color. Almost as important an influence was Nancy Lancaster, an American living in London. "One thing that changed my life singularly was seeing her house in London," says the designer. "She has an extraordinary ability to make a house come to life. But then I do love the way the English live. It's really a sort of comfortable elegance." Indeed, over a decade ago, Mario Buatta gave up his architectural studies at Cooper Union and went with a Parsons study group to Europe. "I've always had a great love for decoration," he continues, "and I was very influenced by everything I saw in Europe—particularly, of course, what I saw in England.

"You know, people often come into my apartment and say, 'Give me a room exactly like this one.' But I really can't. One simply cannot," cautions Mr. Buatta. "It's a very difficult thing to do, because a home is so personal—anyone's home. Duplication is impossible, and entirely unnecessary. I love working with the good pieces people already have.

"I don't feel that decorating is in any way synonymous with fashion," he concludes, "and a superior attitude is a waste of time for a designer. It is the designer's function to help people, to show them what they cannot visualize themselves."

Designer Mario Buatta's New York City apartment mingles urban elegance with country charm. PRECEDING PAGE: In the sprightly Living Room, warm-toned walls backdrop a majestic Queen Anne red-lacquered secretary filled with a collector's harvest of naturalistic faïence. A painted spaniel gazes from its post above the door. RIGHT: Soft lamplight bathes a table-top assemblage that includes Battersea enamel boxes, a ripe porcelain melon and a Regency ivory pagoda.

RIGHT: Floral chintz draperies and pillows extend the country-garden mood of the living room. An English gilt mirror adds sparkle. OPPOSITE: Arranged as precisely as a bouquet, ribbon-suspended chinoiserie mirror paintings balance an 18th-century still life. Centered above, an Adam bracket holds a Chinese blue-and-white vase.

LEFT: *A pair of Rouen pottery dogs perch on a Georgian-style pedimented bookcase in the cozy Bedroom. An 18th-century Chinese Export table functions as a desk. The antique quilt restates the checkerboard pattern of a nearby 18th-century penwork writing cabinet.* BELOW LEFT: *A Regency table holds a convivial grouping of Staffordshire dogs, a sealing wax coffer and a decalcomania-based lamp. An Indian painting glows above.* OPPOSITE: *The painted Sheraton bed offers a chintz-draped haven. The Brighton Pavilion-style chair adds a grace note.*

DESIGN FOR TODAY

In the interiors designed by Arthur Smith the decorator's personality is never obtrusive, and his professional touch is characteristically uninsistent. There is no hint of striving after picturesque effect. Indeed, most of the recognized forms of effect are studiously, almost puritanically, avoided. Color contrasts are subtle, even when the colors used are relatively strong. Elimination is the keynote.

The abiding impression of the Park Avenue duplex that Arthur Smith decorated for two of his clients, a married couple who collect the work of well-known contemporary artists, is that it is exactly as it should be. And it is exactly as the owners wanted it to be: a spacious interior ideally suited to showing their modern paintings. Perhaps more important, they can live in the duplex without feeling as if they were parts of the décor, characters in a play or orphans wandering through a museum.

Mr. Smith is not one to confront or overwhelm a remarkable art collection, but neither is he one to yield to the temptation of matching it. True enough, in the dining room the green of the concentric circles of Kenneth Noland's *Target* is echoed by the green of the upholstered chairs around the table, and in the sitting room the white and black of the sofas suggest that the furniture has been deliberately played down to emphasize Robert Motherwell's emphatically vivid collage above the fireplace. But quite apart from both painting and collage being strong enough to hold their own anywhere without decorative assistance, the Motherwell collage did not yet exist when the apartment was originally decorated. And neither the Noland painting nor any other of the pictures hanging on the walls today formed part of their present owners' collection at that particular time. It seems a minor miracle that all these works of art appear to be quite at home.

"A decorator has to be instinctively prepared for change," says Mr. Smith. "Designing a room is like painting a picture. All the necessary equipment and materials may be there, but unless things are used correctly, the result is a failure. You might compare it with cooking. Two people may start out with the same ingredients, but what they each eventually serve up is never the same. I don't know the secret."

Naturally, he feels the use of color is of the highest importance, as are the placement and design of furniture. He often designs objects and furniture to use in the rooms he decorates. He never ceases to be grateful for the preliminary year he spent studying industrial design at Auburn University before being admitted to the course in interior design for which he had originally been entered. "That year taught me to take in all the facts and to apply the result of the lesson when working out a problem. It was then that I learned how to design anything from a storage cabinet to a cigarette box. And my subsequent years studying interior design taught me how to use my designs effectively within a given space." Mr. Smith's unique skills are especially apparent in the master bedroom, with its soft pastels and muted-toned fabrics, and its combinations of invention and tradition, of discipline and charm.

Some admirable pieces of classic English and French furniture are used in the present apartment, but there is no suggestion that they are being shown off. They simply play an agreeable and natural role —comparable to that played by the various places Arthur Smith has specifically designed for his clients. His distinctive talent is to sense and arrange, unobtrusively and with deceptive ease, precisely what is appropriate in any given situation. It is a talent that creates a feeling of peace and timelessness—an unmistakable Arthur Smith hallmark.

Designer Arthur Smith created a New York City apartment for contemporary art collectors that is as carefully designed as the works of art which it houses.
PRECEDING PAGE: *The Living Room's space-expanding mirrored fireplace wall reflects a Motherwell collage.*

RIGHT: *The designer's inventive use of traditional elements gives the living room a deceptively casual appearance.* Cubistic Flowers, *a Roy Lichtenstein painting, brightens the spacious room; patterned carpeting and textured fabrics add visual interest.*

Precisely balanced elements form a pleasing Living Room arrangement. Stark branches in Chinese-style vases repeat the abstract floral forms of the Lichtenstein painting above.

LEFT: *The Sitting Room is a study in contrasts. A dark chair offsets the rectangle of the fireplace, accenting the crisp geometry of light-and-dark-patterned furnishings. A striking collage by Robert Motherwell is a unifying focal point for the room.*

ABOVE: *Fresh colors and casually comfortable seating create a cheerful Library setting. A jewellike Sam Francis watercolor is prominently displayed before tall bookshelves. A pair of Chinese falcons anchor the low tables that flank the sofa.*

OPPOSITE: *Chamois-textured walls provide an unobtrusive backdrop for a symmetrical dressing-table arrangement in the Master Bedroom. Tissues by Edward Ruscha mysteriously evokes the form of the bench below.*

LEFT: *Gracefully draped printed fabric forms a dramatic ceiling-high canopy over the monumental bed. Elegant and functional bedside tables were created from Chinese coromandel screens.*

LEFT: *The leafy print of the canopy is again used on a wicker chaise longue. The classic paneled walls and mantel are highlighted by a Paul Feeley watercolor and earthenware cachepots.*

A SENSE OF IDENTITY

As women rise to high executive positions in ever-increasing numbers, they are being bombarded with advice. Books and articles abound on how to play sophisticated power games, what sort of briefcase to carry and how to dress with the right combination of elegance and authority. However, no one has said precisely how the single woman with an active professional and social life should design her living space. There is, of course, the old Hollywood stereotype: those glossy penthouse rooms through which Bette Davis or Susan Hayward stalked, casting stalwart shadows on white, pleated lampshades and staring through rain-streaked windows. Successful, but entirely alone.

Much closer to contemporary New York City reality, however, is the compact space that interior designer Robert Metzger has fashioned out of an initially unpromising set of rooms in a relatively new building in Manhattan. "My client and I are old, old friends, so I knew exactly what she wanted."

She was single, involved in a very enjoyable job, and she wanted rooms that were livable without being arch or fussy. "Let's throw out that old cliché about freedom of maintenance," declares the designer. "Isn't that what everybody says when they talk about doing a space for a professional person? My first priority was simply to give a dear friend a home with a sense of her own identity."

What Mr. Metzger has created is what he sought to achieve. Reality was the order of the day. Everything is precisely what it appears to be; there is never the illusion of being in other than a Manhattan apartment of modest scale. There are antiques; but they are agreeable domestic objects, rather than altarpieces ripped out of Portuguese monasteries or painted allegories transplanted from the ceilings of elaborate Renaissance palaces.

The designer has clear ideas about the décor necessary for leading the single life: "You don't need a lot of space when you're alone," he stresses, "but every inch you do have must be intelligently used. In this apartment, every room is essential. I've even managed to conjure up a dining room out of thin air! And then there's vanity. It affects men quite as much as women. Which is why I'm acutely conscious of lighting. To me a centralized fixture—even if it's as diffused as a chandelier—is deadly. It would make a baby look forty."

He is a designer who believes in understanding his clients as much as possible. "I always arrange the first interview in my own apartment. And I never forget that every project is a joint exploration between me and those who choose me to design for their way of life. But let's be reasonable: I see more fabrics and furniture in a week than most people see in a whole lifetime. So it's not surprising that I can appraise a room at a glance.

"Of course, design is something far more intangible," continues Mr. Metzger. "Do you know what I think is the real root of the designing impulse? I think it's a desire to be liked. There are magical times in the relationship between a designer and his client, and moments of sheer hell. But ultimately it is a working friendship. I feel I often know more about my clients than their best friends do."

This clear evaluation of the psychological structure of interior design accounts for a great part of the interest of a Metzger-designed space. "I'm not at all trying to set up bold angles and chic juxtapositions," he explains. "What I'm really about is people's lives and their reaction to an intimate and fluid situation—what is commonly called domestic life. I say to clients, 'You're living here; you've got to *love* it.' Fortunately, most of them do."

Designer Robert Metzger has combined contemporary and traditional elements in this New York City apartment. PRECEDING PAGE: A Clarence Carter painting combining flat patterns and open vistas creates an illusion of space above a console in the Living Room.

BELOW: Silhouetted foliage frames a view of the living room, where a dynamic blend of contrasting styles includes a colorful durrie rug, a bold Soulages painting and delicate paired Louis XVI fauteuils. A Lucite sculpture by Eversley hovers eerily before the windows.

The mirrored wall of the Dining Room reflects the organic form of a Barbara Hepworth sculpture. Indirect lighting casts a soft glow on a Milton Avery painting and velvet-upholstered walls and banquettes. An Art Déco rug restates the shape of the glass-topped table.

OPPOSITE: *A dramatically placed plant atop an antique pedestal overlooks the comfortable seating arrangement in the eclectically appointed bedroom. A multipurpose Louis XV kidney table is a versatile addition to the room.*

DESIGN IN BLACK AND WHITE

Good design is first and foremost the expression of an organizing impulse. It has to do with the imposing of a will upon amorphousness. And it should be a persuasive argument for the virtues of clarity and intelligence. Joseph D'Urso is an interior designer whose work embodies these principles to an unusual degree. His sensibility has a depth of focus that combines uncorrupted forms with a rare sensitivity toward materials. The result has been a series of works of increasing refinement. "I'm interested in the consequences of decisions," he says. "I like the idea of things at their maximum. I think a table, for example, should be as large as possible. The goal is to achieve dynamic proportions, which often establish an architectural quality that hasn't previously existed in the space you're working with."

This duplex apartment that he completed on New York City's West Side, however, did have architecture of a sort. The double-storied living room — twenty-seven by thirty feet — was encased in a shell of dark-stained pine paneling typical of the pseudo-Elizabethan style of many studio buildings that went up in the vicinity of Central Park in the 1920s. "There was no question that the paneling was to be painted white," says Mr. D'Urso. "My first priority was to activate the light." The next step was to transform what had been an extremely fragmented space into a fully integrated one. "When I first went to see the owners," he explains, "I noticed that the family tended to gravitate toward the fireplace, treating it as the center of the room. But, in fact, it is awkwardly placed, in the southeast corner, and can't function as a galvanizing element in the space. Another problem was that the lower sill of the great window facing the skyline was forty-eight inches above the floor. So from a sitting position, the view was totally blocked. It was like being in a pit."

The solution was to build a platform. In a characteristically bold and complete gesture, the designer decreed a massive wedge flush with the window's lower sill and running the whole width of the room at its northern end. Banked with comfortable seating and equipped with tables and lamps, this single structure gives the entire room a center of energy. The absoluteness of the platform is typical of Mr. D'Urso's point of view. It reflects the essential paradox of his work, a spare system of forms that yields great freedom in a disciplined context. The soberness and neutrality of the materials he uses contribute greatly to this end. Gray industrial carpeting and black duck fabric for seating and a rectangle of diamond-plate steel in front of the fireplace are limiting elements that nevertheless allow the individual to blossom with intensity.

"I like to introduce a certain flexibility into my work," points out the designer. "In this case, there are pieces that work in different ways but that always conform to a given order. It's like a game, with an almost unlimited number of resolutions."

To spend time with Joseph D'Urso and to understand the nature of his point of view can be a most rewarding experience. His singularity of purpose and his intellectual strength are balanced by an ingenuous sense of wonder and a dry wit that addresses itself openly to today's design problems.

He also possesses the talent to say exactly what he feels without giving offense. Honesty is important to him, and there is little that is esoteric about his point of view. "Design is simple enough," he says. "It has to do with analyzing the good and the bad and then making certain critical changes." Mr. D'Urso makes great design sound remarkably easy. But the magnificently controlled complexity of his work is eloquent proof that it is not.

PRECEDING PAGE AND ABOVE: *Using boldly contrasting lights and darks, designer Joseph D'Urso created an airy contemporary space in a turn-of-the-century New York City apartment. The platform in the Living Room provides a comfortable seating arrangement for skyline viewing.*

Dark carpeting and upholstery provide a neutral background for bright flowers and greenery in the Living Room. The banked seating area, with its generous pillows, is an inviting center for family gatherings, as well as a perfect focal point for more formal occasions.

OPPOSITE ABOVE: *The Living Room's pristine enameled paneling frames a view of the dining room.* OPPOSITE BELOW: *Mirror-lined niches extend the space in the vaulted Dining Room. Interchangeable table panels can be used for dining or as a practical work surface. When hung on a wall, each dark rectangle resembles a monumental Ad Reinhardt painting.* RIGHT: *The paneled Master Bedroom, a balcony, seems to float above the living room. The owners' children created the lively artwork in the apartment.*

A MIXTURE OF PERIODS

For one designer from a fashion background and another from an interior design background to find that they share a taste for Renaissance furniture is somewhat of a coincidence. To find that the couple who are their nearest personal friends share the same taste suggests unusual good luck. But for the friends of the designers to become clients, and for the four of them to realize an interior that gives full range to their talent and imagination, is virtually a miracle — the kind that could only happen in a Manhattan penthouse high above Central Park.

Interior designers Burt Wayne and John Doktor spent two years searching out the ideal "house in the sky" for their friends before discovering an ideal penthouse surrounded by garden-sized terraces and the essential view of the park. The magnificently proportioned living room offered four evenly placed terrace doors that looked out on what has now become a lush profusion of vegetation punctuated by glorious potted flowers.

Despite a unique kind of balance in the apartment's physical layout, a number of stumbling blocks were there. "A good deal of work had to be done on the closets," points out Mr. Doktor, "because there weren't any. To solve that problem, we built out. Space was at a premium, and everything had to be fitted within an inch of its life."

Happily, the furnishings presented virtually no problems. Designers and owners believed in an identical principle: "If it deviates from the contemporary, then it's Renaissance." They believe in no particular design rules, in any accepted sense. "There is no such thing as something being 'in' or 'out,' " says Mr. Wayne. "Used properly, anything is valid. It can't be said that a French room is more valid than an English one or that an English room is more valid than a contemporary one. We live

in the twentieth century and should live by that standard. The use of suede, steel and glass is largely a twentieth-century approach. But I do feel that Renaissance furniture has the same strength and bulk as contemporary, and its wood gives a nice warmth you don't usually find in the completely contemporary." John Doktor agrees, stating, "My first enthusiasm, while studying at the Parsons School of Design, was French. Then English, then contemporary—and finally Renaissance. Renaissance is an honest kind of furniture. I like the richness of the wood and the carving, and it works well with glass and steel. It is definitely a universal style."

The forthright mixture of Renaissance and contemporary in the penthouse is filled out with the owners' diverse collections picked up in the course of their travels, objects collected for their individual appeal rather than for any special value attached to them. But they interact in a way that is personal and exciting, and they make the somewhat empty interiors dramatic. "The furniture and objects are remarkable," says Burt Wayne, "but the design really isn't a furniture one. If anything, it's a 'mood,' one that is characteristic of our friends. It conforms to their needs, and it was our task to fulfill those needs."

Part of the feeling the owners wanted was a suggestion of a European country house, and the penthouse does have a flavor reminiscent of the farmlands outside Paris or the hills of northern Italy. It is a flavor of contrasts, of the play of delicate fabrics against carved Renaissance wood. Fabrics and periods seem to melt into one another, with mixtures of stucco and tapestry, of whitewash and patterned carpet, of unexpectedly complementary textures. Paradoxically, the décor has great richness and no pretensions, for what has been achieved is the transcription of a highly personal mood.

PRECEDING PAGE: *An ingenious mixture of distinct styles creates an overall mood ideally suited to the Manhattan "house in the sky" that interior designers Burt Wayne and John Doktor found and fashioned for close friends.* RIGHT: *Palladian doors open to a parklike wraparound terrace that filters the businesslike cityscape.* BELOW: *White stucco walls and paintings by South American artists give the spacious Living Room the air of a contemporary hacienda. An opulent rock crystal and amethyst chandelier and a French chair and Italian desk—both 17th century —blend easily with stainless steel cubes, plexiglass console and white leather chairs.* OPPOSITE: *Warm paisley fabric covers the Sitting/Dining Room's walls, ceiling and banquette, echoing the elaborate tracery of carved fruitwood doors and the overdoor panel of iron scrollwork.*

LEFT: *An aura of Old World richness distinguishes the Master Bedroom. Faux tortoiseshell crown molding accentuates the whitewashed walls and sandpainted terra-cotta ceiling; the intricate patterns of luxuriant embroidered pillows and silk patchwork bed coverlet are balanced by an orderly collection of 18th-century architectural drawings. A desk chair covered in 17th-century needlepoint serves as foil for a suede-upholstered Louis XV fauteuil.* ABOVE: *Closet doors done in Aubusson tapestry heighten the European feeling.*

SUTTON PLACE PANORAMA

Interior designer Joseph Braswell almost glows with contentment as he describes life in his new apartment three hundred feet above Sutton Place. "It's been my nature to move on, to tire of a place almost as soon as it is perfected. But I think I'll be living here for a good long time. This apartment has everything I need. It's a haven, compact and serene."

He found this safe harbor in 1974, but it took him nearly two years to complete the décor. For six months he lived with nothing more than a bed and a table, but he accepted his Spartan discomforts in return for the advantages of thinking unhurriedly about how to meet a provocative design challenge. At the center of his plan was the spectacular vista that had drawn him to the building in the first place: a panorama that includes the delicate cat's cradle of the Queensboro Bridge and the bustling East River. With this view as a start, he decided to strike out in an ultracontemporary direction.

Since the building was modern in its basics, and he was merely renting, Mr. Braswell chose not to make any major alterations. Thus he installed track lighting everywhere and designed an integrated system of cabinets and bookshelves that, while appearing architectural in their massiveness, are actually freestanding. "Ordinarily," he points out, "I would drop the ceiling and put in recessed lights. But here, with a concrete slab overhead, the only workable solution was track lighting. It's perfectly flexible, and with a mixture of floods and spots and dimmers I can change both quantity and quality of light almost instantly, even while the guests are on their way up in the elevator. As for the storage wall, that was one of those experiments that, as a designer, I like to try myself before putting it into a client's house. Fortunately, the system I developed with my partner, Ward Willoughby, worked without a hitch."

The idea is inventively simple. The uprights are an ingeniously devised series of wood fins made of matte-finished ash and anchored top and bottom, floor and ceiling, by steel pins. Within the fins each cabinet, finished by contrast in white lacquer, trundles out on casters and can be used as a separate piece.

The play of noncolors in the furniture leads the designer to discuss his personal philosophy: "In our work at Braswell-Willoughby," the designer explains, "we are steeped in strong patterns and colors all day long, and it's easy to become surfeited. Here at home I wanted to restore myself in a tranquil palette of earth tones." The goal has been achieved through a series of counterpoints. The floors are a wall-to-wall expanse of rough-textured, sand-colored sisal; much of the furniture is done in a flawless lacquer of his own devising. Other pieces are of chrome, with minor chords of sensuous suede, silky leather, earthy hopsacking and bright, brittle mirror.

Nevertheless, Mr. Braswell's apartment, for all its crisp modern elements, is a repository for some marvelous curios that reflect his deep interest in tradition, particularly in the eighteenth century. Certainly the grandest of these, in terms of size, is the six-foot-high oak cabinet that dominates one end of the living room. It is a fascinating warren of drawers and doors designed for architectural tools. Of quite different character are the starkly beautiful clay masks, ceremonial gear for some Balinese ritual, that become the focus of another wall. The designer provided the hanging space for them before he had any notion of what would be displayed. As it turned out, he found the right decoration in the shopping arcade of the United Nations Plaza. These unpainted terra-cotta masks add yet another interesting texture to Joseph Braswell's personal and uncommonly shipshape design for living.

Designer Joseph Braswell's New York City apartment is a graceful summation of his informal yet refined design concepts. PRECEDING PAGE: *An Art Déco console balances a fanlike wicker chair, while the foreground bristles with an unusual collection of antique canes.*

BELOW: *The Living Room study area's natural ash wall system contrasts with the shiny smoothness of shelf and desk surfaces. Balinese masks ascending a mirrored wall and an ostrich egg collection add artful touches. The paper sculpture on the wall is by Nancy Miller.*

*L-shaped banquette seating in the Living Room provides
a place for intimate dining and also offers a vantage point
for admiring the spectacular panorama. Eighteenth-
century English suede-upholstered armchairs blend with
the wood tones of a small French mahogany table.*

BELOW AND RIGHT: *A mirror-lined cabinet houses a collection of antique greyhound and whippet pieces. In the Living Room, a greyhound sculpture is silhouetted against the window, with the Queensboro Bridge beyond.*

RIGHT: *Carefully orchestrated neutral colors distinguish the living room's library area. Deep leather-upholstered chairs, inspired by Le Corbusier, form a conversation grouping. An antique English folding library ladder offers easy access to the bookcase.*

The monochromatic Bedroom gains texture from natural cotton bedhangings and handcrafted ash louvered doors. The mirrored wall behind the bed reflects a view of an 18th-century architect's cabinet in the next room.

THE PAST REAFFIRMED

One of the major criticisms leveled at traditional interior design is that there are inherently rigid and unmanageable elements in rooms decorated literally, according to period canons of taste. Keith Irvine and Tom Fleming are two designers whose work makes a good argument to the contrary.

The work they completed on one Park Avenue apartment carries off the seemingly impossible feat of marrying authenticity to flexibility. It is all done with great skill, and perhaps a little leverage. But then, as Keith Irvine puts it, "Most of our work is done for people who have extraordinary attics and basements. We do a lot of pillaging." The owner of this particular apartment was not only the possessor of a number of well-stocked attics, but she was also about to part with a large house in the country and a small pied-à-terre in Manhattan. Thus, there was an embarrassment of riches to work with — a situation that naturally pleased the designers.

"Obviously, we've always worked in a traditional vein," says Tom Fleming. "But we've never allowed that to interfere with our interest in lightness and in what I suppose might be called a sort of ease in the placement of furniture and objects. We've often been called upon to do spaces that were quite theatrical and, if not exactly temporary, certainly not intended for a lifetime. So it was a luxurious moment when our client told us that she saw herself living in this apartment for a good many years." Given the nature of her interests — she is active in the New York museum world, and she needs both work space and room to entertain — the two designers decided to abandon the functional role that is usually allotted to conventional rooms.

The foyer sounds the theme immediately: Entered from the mirrored hall, it is really a kind of prefatory living room, complete with comfortable seating and a reproduction of a complex Chinese wallpaper. The authoritative note of the living room is unique in the generally relaxed context of the apartment. "The owner believes there are moments when a less approachable splendor is in order," says Mr. Fleming. Thus, the furniture in the living room is arranged in solemn hieratic configurations, and there is a sense of distance not found in the other rooms.

One means of avoiding any possible monotony in the design of period rooms is to constantly seek new ways of presenting familiar scenes. In a bedroom that has all the languishing romanticism of a Verdi aria, there are walls of sumptuous depth and paleness. Literally watercolors painted onto the plaster, they turn the room into a mysterious iridescent container. "Most of the people who come to us are connected to one another by birth or friendship," explains Mr. Fleming. "And they do understand fine things. Keith likes to say that they use our experience to give some authority to what they could really do themselves. However, I like to think that knowledge gives our work a depth and an edge that only professionals can achieve."

Perhaps it is this sense of fastidiousness that is most apparent in an Irvine-Fleming interior — a perfection of finish carried to an assured point, never becoming glazed or apathetic, but always alert and always executed with the slightest suggestion of irony and wit. There is never anything that strikes the eye as being pompous or academic. The people of the past were living, it must be remembered, in homes and not museums. And if Mr. Irvine and Mr. Fleming are happiest with the décor of that past, they still manage to approach it with a delightful mixture of irreverence and respect. It is the perfect way to carry out the dictates of traditional design and still remain in the spirit of the twentieth century.

Interior designers Keith Irvine and Thomas Fleming combined the elegance of the traditional with a refreshing note of unconventionality in this Park Avenue apartment. PRECEDING PAGE: *In the Entrance Hall, a Chinese wicker giraffe, apparently enjoying the fragrance of fresh blossoms, stands atop a painted Louis XVI console.*

ABOVE AND RIGHT: *The bold pattern of a 19th-century Bessarabian rug underscores the rich mixture of colors and textures in the Living Room. The painting above the sofa is by Gerod deLain; an Italian wood and crystal chandelier and the symmetrical arrangement of a Louis XVI gilt-framed mirror flanked by delicate watercolors add subtle finishing touches to the tableau.*

The vibrant hues of the Dining Room/Library both unify the room and infuse it with a cheerful warmth. The display of books and objets d'art is backed by glossy Chinese red lacquer. The pale rug and the deep-toned sofa are like pools of shade in the sunny surroundings.

The Dining Room/Library emphasizes comfort and relaxation. A sofa covered in a lively print fabric is an unusual companion for the Chippendale chairs attending the 18th-century mahogany dining table. A painting of horses by Jean Vinay sets off a brilliant lacquered wall.

BELOW: *Cascades of sheer eyelet drape the canopied bed in the Master Bedroom. Dainty French petit-point carpeting, chintz draperies and matching chaise, and a bed coverlet sprigged with roses and ribbons complete a picture of graceful refinement.* RIGHT: *A pair of Hepple-white mahogany beds are canopied with bright French gingham in the Guest Room. A floral painting and floral print draperies add to the feeling of youthful gaiety.*

A MINIMAL APPROACH

Less is less, and more is a bore. Such are the two prevailing ironic attitudes toward the opposite poles of interior design today. The serious question is how much can be subtracted from anything without ending up with nothing? And how much can be added without total confusion? The middle road of compromise might offer a practical solution to some, but not to Anthony Tyson. His East Side apartment in Manhattan settles for a lot less than less—and still manages to provide more.

A designer of luxurious but minimal shapes in furniture, he depends mostly on superb finish and detailing that may go unnoticed by the casual observer. "I'm a perfectionist," he explains, "and I love detail." Once a dealer in American antiques, he owns superb examples of Early American furniture and painting. "I do feel very strongly about American things. At one point, I had an antiques shop in Quogue, on Long Island, and I still look for fine pieces on my travels. I don't hesitate to add them to the apartment." Nevertheless, he uses these objects sparingly, giving each its own space and distance. A sense of placement is one of the highest achievements of his design talent.

That talent, of course, has not been acquired instantly. But even in a former apartment of his, in New York's SoHo, the designer's sense of placement was already extraordinarily sophisticated. A respect for architectural quality and the integrity of buildings of the past motivated Mr. Tyson in the interior arrangement of his present apartment, farther uptown in Manhattan. His is a floor-through apartment in a converted turn-of-the-century mansion, once a private townhouse.

The twenty-five-foot-square living room is a compelling example of simplicity achieved without starkness—a simplicity that breathes its own particular brand of richness. The effects are far from complicated. Basically there is one sofa, one rug, one picture. Three windows break up the rhythm of solitaire, as do pairs of chairs and low tables and a cluster of dining room furniture. Even so, the general atmosphere is not stark; sets of decorative objects enliven the room, including two Whieldon pots on the sofa table, three original American Hepplewhite painted chairs, a pair of antique Korean tea tables used for cocktails and—in a niche housing a collection of Baccarat—several Leeds pots. The one painting is a superb American Primitive.

"I don't believe that one thing should be shouldered against another, simply to make everything come together," says the designer. "Each thing in a room must be given its own particular integrity." He follows his design point of view to the letter. The entrance hall, for example, has been stripped down to the imitation-stone plasterwork, and in it are a pair of fine seventeenth-century Connecticut Valley Flemish scroll chairs and a William and Mary looking glass. An American Primitive, circa 1850, with a curious double profile, enlivens the Williamsburg whitewashed walls that have been textured with Tampico brushwork. Other rooms in the three-thousand-square-foot apartment have a similar thrust, though the decorative effects do differ.

"I sincerely believe that architects today are involved with interiors as architecture, rather than as decoration," says Mr. Tyson. "There is a movement away from the cluttered look. This is true not only in domestic architecture but in restaurants and other commercial spaces." He feels quite strongly that at the present moment this newfound simplicity is achieved for visual reasons, rather than for any reasons of functionalism. His own apartment in New York City is an excellent illustration.

Anthony Tyson's treatment of space as an architectural form creates a boldly dramatic interior in his Manhattan apartment. PRECEDING PAGE: The spare use of furnishings in the Living Room enhances the total effect of height and light. Low Korean tables add dark accents.

Each object in the Living Room projects its presence through careful placement. Mahogany wainscoting forms a ribbonlike band around the walls. Works of art include a pair of Whieldon ceramic urns and a 19th-century primitive painting attributed to Ezra Ames.

OPPOSITE: *A sunburst of shirred theatrical gauze radiates across the ceiling of the Bedroom. The same fabric is used for the Tyson-designed high bed and the arched window above the door. Walls are covered with Philippine handmade paper, producing a subtle geometric note in the background. An 18th-century American banister-back chair adds a prim touch to the airy lightness of the room.*

METROPOLITAN DECOR

One of the most difficult and consistently elusive feats of interior design is to work with restraint, and even delicacy, on a generous budget. Simplicity, even austerity, within the context of perfect workmanship and luxurious materials, is a rarity. Yet how completely satisfying it is to walk into such a space. And how immediate and how unmistakably right it always seems. To know that the constraint was self-imposed and to feel the balance and harmony that obviously prevail between client and interior designer are equally pleasing. All these elements are present in the comparatively small apartment high in the Olympic Tower in Manhattan that Melvin Dwork designed for "dear friends."

To spend any time at all in the space is to subtly but conclusively revise the personal meaning of the word *luxury*. A world of exquisitely plain surfaces unfolds, and materials defer in an almost Oriental fashion to the Babylonian splendor of the view. From a vantage point of over four hundred feet, the ziggurats and worldly temples of New York City look almost barbaric, while immediately below the Gothic fretwork of the topmost spires of Saint Patrick's Cathedral dissolve into fragile lace. It is awe-inspiring and is scarcely filtered out by the tinted glass of the apartment's outer perimeter. It is typical of Mr. Dwork's design that this aggressive panorama is made to work within the context of a series of rooms that neither defer to the view nor ignore it.

"The basic problem of contemporary construction in this country," says Mr. Dwork, "really comes down to proportions. Luckily, this building was completed to exceptional standards, so I had a little room in which to maneuver. Ceilings are slightly higher than average, for example, and windows come right down to the floor. Of course, the latter is a rather double-edged joy. The windows admit light and the view, but they all too often feel psychologically terrifying." His solution is elegantly simple. In the living room, a shelf of thick plate glass, sixteen feet long by thirty-six inches wide, runs along the west windows, while a diplomatically placed sofa screens the southern exposures. Columns are redefined by being sheathed in gray-tinted solar glass, which also serves to conceal the impressive lighting and sound systems, so much a feature of the designer's sensibility. "In this case I think I detailed the columns quite ingeniously," he says, pointing to the crisp mirrored slots that direct a fine-grained ray of light into the apartment.

Superb and flamboyant Renaissance pieces recur throughout the apartment. In the bedroom a vast and confident armoire is a commanding presence. And it is here that Mr. Dwork's clients keep a few delicately scaled sculptures, to take out occasionally and savor in the manner of the Japanese who believe that to display an object constantly is to drain it of its force and beauty. Such a tactful and sensitive gesture is almost a metaphor for the whole space and for the understanding between clients and designer. A sybaritic daybed intercepts the view from the window and is approached via a small platform. This detail is one of the most subtle points in the apartment. It serves to place the reckless view on a sort of elegant platter, but at the same time — by effectively lowering the ceiling — makes it feel paradoxically safe. All the same, some would undoubtedly consider it a daring feat to recline on this couch while, far below, the endless flotillas of Fifth Avenue traffic move noiselessly forward.

The most moving aspect of the space is its silent endorsement of that blend of restraint and luxury that is so vital to the modern temperament, and so masterfully realized in the work of Melvin Dwork.

Designer Melvin Dwork created a New York City apartment that utilizes a spectacular view of the Manhattan
skyline as its dominant element. PRECEDING PAGE: Solar-
gray mirrored walls and pale velvet upholstery give the
Living Room an air of neutral tranquillity.

In the Living Room, modern elements and antique objects are carefully juxtaposed. A glass shelf along the length of a wall visually underlines the view. In the foreground, a 17th-century Italian table holds amaryllis and a photographic floral study by Peter Fink.

OPPOSITE: *In the Master Bedroom, an elevated window seat bridging the floor-to-ceiling window is a vantage point for viewing the stunning Manhattan panorama.*

LEFT: *The master bedroom's pale silk wallcovering and upholstery of hand-woven wool create a harmony of subtle textures. Two 17th-century Dutch chairs lend a note of antique charm.*

FAR LEFT: *A massive 17th-century South German armoire is a commanding presence in the master bedroom.* LEFT: *A custom-designed plexiglass basin and mirror, accented by brass fittings, gleam in the contemporary Master Bath.*

URBAN ELEGANCE

It calls attention to itself simply because it is beautiful and full of beautiful objects. The Manhattan apartment of Michael Lynch is the splendid end result of a somewhat unusual teacher/student relationship in the field of interior design.

Several years ago Michael Lynch acquired a five-room penthouse cooperative on New York's Upper East Side and started to work with interior designer Kevin McNamara to decorate the apartment. The two had first met several years before when Mr. McNamara was associated with Parish-Hadley, the interior design firm that had done Mr. Lynch's first New York apartment. At the time, Michael Lynch was studying art history at Columbia; but he decided to change careers and went to work as an assistant to Kevin McNamara, who was in the process of opening his own firm. Thus, with the help of Mr. McNamara, he gained professional knowledge that might otherwise have taken years to acquire. However, in the present apartment, there is no indication that one was the leader, the other the follower. There was a conscious blurring of roles.

"Kevin guided me," explains Mr. Lynch. "I took my directions from him, but I wasn't really a client. I have some very good collections of china and French furniture, but I didn't want the apartment to look like a museum. I don't like the cold and sterile look that the houses of some collectors have. My things are special, certainly, but not so unique that they need to be displayed as if they were museum pieces. I want to live in the present, not the past."

His is now an environment in which ambience transcends mere decoration. The rooms have a certain ease and friendliness about them, exactly the look and the feeling both owner and designer wished to achieve. "Comfort was a most important consideration," says Mr. Lynch. "I made it a point, since I didn't want to be distracted by my possessions. Perhaps more than anything else, I care for personal comfort." Indeed, there is comfort in the apartment—and there is color in abundance, as well. Color, a McNamara trademark, is found both in the selection of luxurious fabrics and in the paint itself, strongly unifying the apartment and linking one room to the other. Plump pillows and tables are within reach, and conversation areas merge successfully to make this residence a most pleasant place.

If any man is surrounded by the belongings he loves, it is Michael Lynch. Everywhere the eye turns, a lovely work of art is seen. The art, contributing a dramatic aura to the apartment, includes four signed Louis XVI chairs, Greek sculpture and a Sung bronze. "These are just the things I personally love and love to have around me," states Mr. Lynch. "In a very real sense, I think of myself as a guardian. I only wish some of these things could talk! I suppose I've always been a collector. Everyone in my family—my parents, my sister, my aunts—collects Early American furniture. So you see, I *had* to collect something else, something completely different."

Despite the many rare objects, an elegant simplicity permeates the living room. Flooded with natural light during the day, its walls are coated with lacquer—a marvelous ivory shade, the color of a Carr's water biscuit. "But the room is actually more effective at night," observes Mr. Lynch. "Especially on a winter's night when the fire is flickering, the candles are lit, flowers are arranged and people are gathered together. Then it's glorious."

Kevin McNamara, a designer consistently aware of what makes a room beautiful, agrees, indicating that the living room is his favorite. "There are no set rules. I personally feel the magic happens when people have the things they love around them."

PRECEDING PAGE: *Michael Lynch collaborated with designer Kevin McNamara to create an understated setting for the collections of treasured objects that grace his New York City apartment.* BELOW: *Deep-toned walls and book-lined étagères provide a warm atmosphere in a Dining Room that doubles as a Library. The 18th-century dining table is Louis XVI.*

OPPOSITE LEFT: *Light-hued walls provide a neutral backdrop for a Bessarabian rug and Japanese crane panels.* OPPOSITE RIGHT: *The Living Room's herringbone-patterned wood floor underscores a Boulle cabinet filled with Chinese porcelains. A 1st-century Roman sculpture tops an 18th-century French table.* OPPOSITE BELOW: *The dining room radiates vitality, from the marble-manteled fireplace to the contemporary painting by George Dahl.*

RIGHT: *A richly patterned Chinese rug and a graceful Italian bronze deer animate the Master Bedroom. Linear paintings are by George Dahl.* BELOW: *The simplicity of the raw-silk-canopied bed contrasts with richly colored walls in the master bedroom. A Louis XVI table holds photos and cherished mementos. An Anthony Thieme boatscape and inlaid hexagonal mirrors adorn the walls.*

In the handsomely appointed Guest Room, works of art from different eras coexist harmoniously. A 17th-century Khmer sculpture rests on an early-19th-century Japanese diaper-motif lacquer chest, counterpointing a dignified Egyptian bronze cat perched atop the mirrored Louis XVI desk.

FLUIDITY OF SPACE

Richard Giglio cannot remember a time when he was not in the habit of drawing or painting virtually every object in sight. Today, in his early forties, he is an accomplished artist—a fluent draftsman and a sensitive colorist. These are qualities apparent not only in his art but in his life, as well.

He has the rare good fortune to live in what is, for an artist, the ideal New York apartment. It is at the top of interior designer Angelo Donghia's handsome private house in Manhattan's East Seventies. The apartment consists principally of a living room and a studio. They are both relatively modest in proportion but filled with daylight that comes from three sizable windows in each room, with ample views unimpeded by neighboring high-rise buildings. There is also a third room, upstairs, that serves as an alternate studio when the artist is working on larger paintings. Outside each studio is a terrace, and both are used as roof gardens, as outdoor dining rooms and for alfresco work.

Since Mr. Giglio is in the habit of moving his furniture and objects around from one day to the next, it is difficult to describe the precise arrangement of the apartment at any particular juncture. More to the point would be a mention of those characteristics and components of the interior that are not temporary, but endemic. This is a place designed for both living and working. But even though it has the warmth and interest of possessions admired for their personal associations, it is clean and uncluttered. The painting boards and artist's materials are neatly arranged in a former clothes closet, from which Mr. Giglio has removed the doors. Tall and unwieldy rolls of his favorite "detail paper" are kept well under control, and even provide an attractive design element, in two large French cement garden pots.

He likes books, but he does not leave them on the shelves to be forgotten and gather dust. Instead, he keeps many of them on his tables, lying open at a favorite illustration, or stacks them firmly on the floor and uses the piles as extra tables. Among other substitutes for tabletops are a fine Venetian mirror, a painting board set on a French iron garden-table base and the seats of chairs. Even when the artist uses a normal table, he is likely to have "made it my own" by painting it black or cutting down its legs. Actually, the nearest approach to luxury in the apartment is the sofa bed in the living room. It is a focal point, a pivot around which all else moves, or is periodically moved. Designed by the artist some years ago, it is a temple of ease, with high backs and sides and a chaos of cushions, all covered in pale gray quilting. Yet for all its unashamed comfort and monumental proportions, it fits admirably into its surroundings. For, mysteriously, there is a perceptible undercurrent of abundance in the atmosphere of this superficially simple interior. It can make sensual magic just as well out of a stack of books, a row of tangerines above the fireplace or three paper fans in a terra-cotta pot.

Inevitably, these two rooms—arranged, rearranged, lived in and worked in by an artist—reveal an aspect or two about their owner's character and tastes. Less expectedly, they also provide an accurate preview and a rewarding echo of his art—and not just because of those particular drawings and paintings by the artist that happen to be there at a given time. The combination of white walls, pale gray bed, black accents and delicate color patches constitutes, in its different medium, a spectrum identical to the spectrum of Richard Giglio's present work. All has come full circle, and, in his home, the interdependence of art and life seems complete.

PRECEDING PAGE: *Richard Giglio's New York City apartment combines an artist's creativity with a zest for living. A 1928 Bonfils poster in the Living Room acts as the foil for one of Giglio's own paintings, displayed above the multipillowed quilted sofa bed.*

BELOW LEFT: *An ever-changing mélange of interesting objects and evocative natural forms inspires the artist. The living room has become an ongoing display of his and others' works. A Matisse reproduction adds an animated note to the tabletop assortment.*

ABOVE AND OPPOSITE: *Other views of the living room reveal the multipurpose fabric-draped table holding books and one-of-a-kind objects. Amaryllis and stark quince branches in Art Déco vases make dramatic statements. Works of art surround the fireplace, while a precisely placed row of fruit, in the manner of a Chinese still life, rests on the mantel.*

BELOW: *A jewellike Lalique lamp glows in the daylight-filled Living Room. Stacked art books function also as supports for various objects. A French garden pot contains drawing paper.* BOTTOM: *Works in progress and bright Giglio-designed fabrics fill the cheerful Studio.*

SETTING FOR ART AND ANTIQUES

One of the most subtle challenges an interior designer is likely to meet is that of reworking an existing collection of furniture and art objects into a new environment. For Luis Rey, of McMillen, Inc., in New York City, the challenge was underscored by two problems. The first was quantity. The owners of a newly purchased Park Avenue apartment had a vast and complex collection of botanical prints, of paintings and other objets d'art—holdings too great to fit into a single residence. So editing became a very necessary priority. Quality, paradoxically, was the other problem. Mr. Rey was confronted with the refined and authoritative tastes of the owners, and he had to work within limits imposed by a couple who knew precisely what they wanted. Surely it is a tribute to everyone concerned that the result is an intelligent assessment of the related values of living well, and of living aesthetically.

The beginning of the project for the designer was the consideration of an entire floor in one of those solid Manhattan buildings that were conceived with a life span calculated to run from 1927 ad infinitum and that, architecturally, have more to do with fortifications than with domesticity. Exposures on all four sides of the structure assured the apartment of extraordinary light and views, and its position on a high floor gave it the mysterious, almost transcendent, quality that is unique to Manhattan, and almost indigenous to the East Side. Originally the lowest floor of a triplex, the space divides rather easily into two parts. The rooms facing east were left structurally untouched; but the western half of the apartment, which had been a "warren of servants' rooms," was gutted and reconstructed as bedrooms and baths for the owners and their children. In addition, there were the usual eccentricities so often found in buildings dating from the 1920s: a paneled library, for instance, that had been brought over intact from some dismembered English house and installed two hundred feet above the sidewalks of New York. The prevailing fantasy of that time, of course, was to create a private house within the framework of a huge, steel-framed building.

"And yet the intent was not so very different from what was done in this renovation," explains Mr. Rey. "The most important consideration was that of creating a comfortable and livable space. Although the apartment is full of exquisite and fragile things, I never considered that I was working within the confines of invisible velvet ropes."

Much of the furniture the designer was dealing with had in fact been purchased by the owners some years ago, when they first worked with McMillen. Mrs. Archibald Brown, the founder of McMillen, with her incomparable mixture of firmness and delicacy, was able to persuade the young couple to buy many objects that have stayed with them ever since. "Of course, Mrs. Brown came up to this apartment, too," says Luis Rey, "and naturally she discerned things. She moved a table a few inches here, rehung a picture there. She used her incredible eye for placement to its fullest advantage. Quality is always an expanding experience, and I learned a great deal while doing this apartment. The discrimination required, for example, to select forty prints out of a hundred fine ones is quite sobering.

"I think my approach can really be summed up quite easily," he concludes. "I have an unsentimental and pragmatic point of view. I said, in effect, 'This is what we have, and this is all we're really going to need. Now let's make something out of it.'" What this modest appraisal conceals is a complex, yet very logical, orchestration of time and place—livable and harmonious décor at its best.

PRECEDING PAGE: *Warm-toned walls give a glow to the Elevator Foyer of a New York City apartment designed by Luis Rey. Light filtering through an arched window burnishes a 13th-century bronze Khmer head and creates gleaming reflections on an inlaid Adam demilune table.*

BELOW: *A 13th-century carved wood Kuan Yin introduces a note of serenity in the Entrance Hall, reaffirmed by a 17th-century bronze Sukhothai head gracing a George III mahogany butler's desk. A Louis XVI game table holds pots of flowers; above it is a Daubigny landscape.*

A precisely arranged wall assemblage comprised of colorful botanical prints garnered from Brookshaw's Pomona Britannica (1812) enlivens the Drawing Room. An 18th-century Agra rug and damask floral upholstered Louis XV chairs underscore the room's air of spirited elegance.

The soft-hued Drawing Room provides a gracious
backdrop for groupings of lovingly chosen objets d'art.
Paired K'ang Hsi porcelain birds on the mantel balance a
portrait by Sir Henry Raeburn. Seventeenth-century
Dutch watercolors and Redouté still lifes, arranged with
pleasing symmetry, flank the cheerful fire.

114

Glowing golden hues and an aura of exoticism distinguish the Dining Room. The batik print of the table linen repeats the colors of a Japanese Momoyama bird screen. George III chairs surround the table; their delicacy complements the dramatic setting.

In the bright, springlike Breakfast Room, which opens onto a terrace banked with flowers, a grouping of 18th-century watercolors by Martinet patterns the walls. An open Chinese lacquer parasol above the table filters the overhead lights, adding to the sunny feeling.

LEFT: *Two Louis XVI chairs upholstered in a crisp floral fabric attend a tulipwood commode of the same period in the Master Bedroom.* BELOW LEFT: *Mirrors reflect the rich surfaces of the Master Bath/Dressing Room. The marble-topped vanity, chevron-design ceramic tiling, mottled suede vinyl wallcovering and geometric-patterned carpet merge into a visual symphony of textures. The opulence of the velvet-covered daybed is tempered by an austere print of Trajan's column and a dignified 7th-century Japanese stone head.*

The comfort and coziness of the Master Bedroom are enhanced by a unifying theme of botanical motifs. Small floral prints surround a 17th-century Dutch still life over the bed, while flowered linens restate the delicate bouquets in framed French wallpaper panels.

AN INDIVIDUAL TOUCH

Exuberance and a sense of abandon are qualities much prized in interior design, yet they are intrinsically double-edged. Knowing when to stop, holding off the final effect that mars or cloys, is one of the true tests of a professional.

Yet there is also a perfectly good case to be made for the talented amateur whose taste is so instinctive that it naturally enhances any setting it chooses. Such instinct is gloriously evident in the work of Suzie Frankfurt, who, in fact, has now made the transition from amateur to professional interior designer. From the moment she opens the door of her East Side townhouse, she is completely and engagingly vibrant. Her appearance is an intricate collage of elements — a vaguely Kurdish peasant blouse, combined with a severe black velvet skirt. It is obvious that her design philosophy is principally one of quality. Nothing superficial, or lacking in what she might call "majesty," is permitted in these rooms, paradoxically light in their effect, but densely and intelligently packed with objects. "I like anything that's a little out of the ordinary," she says. "That's why I'll place an eighteenth-century marriage chest from Damascus under an eighteenth-century mirror, top it with a thirteenth-century Tibetan Buddha — and then flank the whole effect with two Japanese military chests."

Almost everything in her eclectic house is three-dimensional or in some way tactile: "I love small sculpture," explains Suzie Frankfurt. "You can pick it up and feel it. It lives. Paintings, on the other hand, just hang on the walls; and you may or may not throw darts at them. I guess you could say that movement is one of my obsessions." Hers is an intensely autobiographical house. Literally dozens of early Andy Warhol drawings testify to a long friendship with the artist, while boiseries from Italy and Spain reflect a passion for travel. "All design is basically personal," she points out. "When you're doing it for someone else you have to be a psychiatrist as well. But when you've analyzed your clients, you can start thinking in terms of what they'd like or need. There is, incidentally, no big black book that says, 'This must be done in a certain way.'" In her own search for the evocative and the unorthodox, she is likely to come up with exquisitely obscure periods and styles: "If you thought my Egyptian-style sleigh bed was authentic," she adds, "you'd be quite wrong. It's actually post-1922 nouveau riche Cairo, and I dug it out of a souk!"

Certain people possess enormous energy and the earthy and mysterious kind of glamour that is pre-Hollywood. Suzie Frankfurt is one of them: "I'm a very academic person," she says in apparent contradiction of the sumptuously theatrical and worldly nature of her living room. "To me there's nothing rigid implied in being academic; it simply means erudition. And that's the basis of everything that's going on in this house." However, she continues, "I want to make the point that I *do* collect. Everything in this house, apart from a few upholstered pieces, is a work of art that appeals to me."

Her philosophy, as with her townhouse, is a wry blend of intelligent insight and the occasional non sequitur: "I like symmetry," she states. "Two of everything or multiples of two. You won't find a single unpaired chair in *this* house."

But there is far more to the art of Suzie Frankfurt than the clever display of learned juxtapositions. "Let me just say that if a person stepped right off the street into my house and, without even knowing me, studied the contents of these rooms, that person would come to a very important realization — that there really is a good deal of knowledge here."

The distinctive Manhattan townhouse of interior
designer Suzie Frunkfurt exhibits the owner's penchant
for collecting. PRECEDING PAGE: An 18th-century
Chinese ancestor portrait gazes down on a Burmese
Buddha and a pair of mother-of-pearl inlaid armchairs in
the Entrance Hall. BELOW: The ornate motif of an inlaid
marriage chest from Damascus repeats the lacy pattern
of the bronze banister, originally part of Hetty Green's
New York bank. BOTTOM: Sculptured heads from various
cultures grace an 18th-century Portuguese gilded table.
RIGHT: In the Parlor, Art Déco chairs and a glass and
steel table counterpoint the Brazilian votive heads,
Egyptian-style daybed and 21st-Dynasty sarcophagus.
A carved wood figure seems to raise a hand in greeting.

OPPOSITE: *An antique chandelier, hung with Baccarat crystal drops, illuminates the Dining Room. Austrian red crystal and Georgian flatware sparkle on the table below, which is surrounded by a collection of Thonet chairs. Two 18th-century paintings and a 19th-century clock punctuate the far wall.* ABOVE RIGHT: *The inviting atmosphere of the Library is underscored by geometric-patterned carpeting. An Egyptian mummy case adorns one wall.* BELOW RIGHT: *Andy Warhol's shoe drawings, circa 1958, add a droll note to the upstairs Hallway.*

Expansive, undraped windows bring the outdoors into the Master Bedroom. A Scott Martin painting, an antique English table that has been lacquered and a child's chair from France add to the air of nostalgia. Daisy-strewn wallcovering and a flower-sprigged eiderdown extend the room's floral motif.

CENTRAL PARK VISTA

"Dedicated to yesterday's charm and tomorrow's convenience"—these words are chiseled in stone outside the Hampshire House, that stately residential hotel on Central Park South. In a number of ways, the motto describes one of the apartments in it: the Leonard Kahn penthouse. Decorated by friend and one-time neighbor Hariet Eckstein, the Kahn cooperative follows the themes of traditional decoration and modern comfort. Updated to reflect today's tastes, the apartment also manages to evoke the aura of a more gracious past.

"An honest and timeless quality is important in decoration," says Ms. Eckstein. "I don't believe that I should simply reproduce this year's fads." She admits to having "backed into decorating" in the late 1950s when her husband started Roundtree, Inc., one of the first firms in the United States to design and manufacture French country reproductions. "People were always coming into the showroom and asking if I were a decorator," she explains. "As an artist, I'd lived my life surrounded by beautiful objects, things that my husband and I loved to collect—like the French furniture. Little by little, I started taking on a few decorating projects."

Two of her early clients were Edith and Leonard Kahn, who lived next door to her on Long Island's North Shore. When they decided to move back to New York City, she was asked to give their penthouse "some wit and charm, and some unexpected touches." Creating an atmosphere to match their outgoing personalities, she designed with gracious living and easy entertainment in mind. A relaxing and luxurious space, the apartment seems to work effortlessly. "I am not at all inflexible," says the designer. "I feel my way as I go along. And I particularly like working with people such as the Kahns, who share my attitude."

The apartment is full of ideas that serve to liberate space. In a sense, every room is a sitting room providing versatility and flow—including the unusual kitchen, a delicious surprise with its intricate chinoiserie inspired by a room that the designer had seen in Paris. In the expansive living room with its view of Central Park, the designer provided the owners with a restful anchorage for their collections of well-loved objects and Impressionist paintings. Formality is underplayed, and the room has a serene and pleasing look, derived in part from paneled walls depicting the four seasons. With so much natural light flooding the room, the designer avoided intense and competitive colors: "The monochromatic scheme has a softening effect that doesn't vie with the view for attention," she points out.

She also created clever seating arrangements—two large sofas with large and comfortable pillows covered in a fabric print of Aesop's fables—so that guests are always close to one another in a banquettelike grouping. At one end of the room, near a floor-to-ceiling glass window, a balcony area has been enlivened with plants. It is an effective and amusing way of bringing Central Park indoors. In a very real way the entire apartment manages to lift the spirit. This is particularly true in the master bedroom, where the designer reversed a Watteau-like fabric and used it throughout the room. The result creates an impression of being inside a large bouquet of flowers. The mirrored bath, with white tile mosaics handpainted by Cele Lord, gives the feeling of walking through some marvelous flower bed.

"It is a great joy for me to help develop someone else's taste," says Hariet Eckstein. "When I leave, the house or apartment I have decorated should keep going. Everything should be used, and that's the whole point. Please *do* touch!"

Eighteenth-century boiserie walls and a handsome
Bessarabian rug augment the traditional spirit of the
Living Room. Near the marble mantel, a Renoir painting
of a bather glows beneath a rock-crystal sconce. A brass
and steel table introduces a modern note.

In a Kitchen that evokes the feeling of an 18th-century sitting room, painted chinoiserie panels conceal the room's utilitarian appliances. The parquet de Versailles flooring repeats the lattice motif. Chippendale and Adam-style furnishings reinforce the 18th-century mood.

A marble and malachite floor in the Dining Room counterpoints a crystal chandelier. On the wall, an ornate Régence mirror hangs above a stately 18th-century commode. Beyond the doorway, a Chinese lacquer cabinet echoes the springlike motif of the wallcovering.

BELOW: *Velvet-covered walls and finely carved moldings provide a gracious setting for the Library's oak bookcases. A rose-splashed English needlepoint rug and an 18th-century Dutch flower study complement a dark lacquer table à écrire. Tortoise chairs are covered in suede.*

In a Master Bedroom that resembles an enchanted bower, a Queen Anne mirror reflects the shirred-silk canopy of the arboreal tester bed. At the foot stands an 18th-century miniature daybed. The whimsical lily-pad chair and floral chintz wallcoverings extend the garden mood.

A VICTORIAN TOWNHOUSE

Even the most relentlessly overbuilt city seems to harbor tiny oases, little clusters of houses that stubbornly resist every effort to dislodge them. They manage to hang on, decade after decade, witnesses to a more delicately scaled way of life. Their mysterious tenacity must have a great deal to do with the love such enclaves inspire in their owners. These neighborhoods attract those intelligent few who understand the need for the subtle to triumph over the obvious, the refined over the coarse.

There is a small row of these houses on Manhattan's East Side that has a particularly felicitous record of survival. It was built in the 1860s for bachelor soldiers returning from the Civil War, and since then its painted, ivy-covered façades have never had to hide the ignominy of subdivision into apartments. The unusual scale of these houses may have had as much to do with their survival as sentiment. Fifteen feet wide and only three stories high, they were virtual dollhouses to the Victorians but are ideally sized for twentieth-century New Yorkers seeking both fine proportions and intimacy.

More than a decade ago, Jay Crawford and Anthony Tortora acquired one of these collector's items and began a long process of exploration and experimentation that culminated in a sophisticated house. No physical alterations were made; through the manipulation of objects alone, Mr. Crawford and Mr. Tortora created a series of spaces in which the art of pure decoration is evident. It is a house at once conservative, luxurious and revolutionary in its use of proportions. It is a house for an intellectual — or a sybarite. The owners are not interior designers by profession. Jay Crawford is a fashion illustrator and Anthony Tortora's partner in Quadrille, a company for which they design fabric and wallpapers with great flair and imagination.

"We wanted a distinctly urban house," says Mr. Crawford. "But at the same time, we wanted it to function like a screen or a filter, shutting out all the noise and tension of the city. And naturally, we wanted to let in all the things that make us confirmed New Yorkers — elegance, energy and marvelous people. We both like to entertain, and the house is very much oriented toward social life."

The living room, situated as it is on the middle level of the house — above the dining room and the kitchen and below the bedrooms and sitting room — serves as a handy paradigm for the whole miniature ensemble. It is not a large space, but the objects in it are dramatically overscaled. "We love palace furniture," says Mr. Tortora disarmingly, "or at least palatial scale." The way pieces designed for different purposes, some of them quite grandiose, have been selected to work in rooms modest even by contemporary standards is part of the special and unusual delight of the house. Though the owners have surrounded themselves with lovely antiques, they have surely not developed a pious attitude.

"A house is meant to be a place where you can put your feet on the furniture or lounge in bed on a Saturday morning," says Jay Crawford. "There is no such thing as luxury here — only necessity."

The power and coherence of the décor as it is now arranged stems as much from its sense of unfettered choice as it does from honesty. The style is bold, coherent and completely without nationality. The house embraces many ways of seeing, yet everything seems to work harmoniously together. It is free of conventional Western ideas of scale, offering an ambience in which a sophisticated person from any culture might feel comfortable. Such is the secret of complete modernity and a happy augury for the continuing existence of charm and good taste.

Grandly scaled furnishings fill the high-ceilinged Victorian spaces of Jay Crawford and Anthony Tortora's New York City townhouse. PRECEDING PAGE: *The eclectic mood of the Living Room is emphasized by a Claudio Bravo trompe l'oeil painting, an austere window treatment and the artistic owners' patterned fabrics.*

BELOW LEFT AND RIGHT: *Objets d'art garnered from many cultures form intriguing still lifes in the Hallway.* OPPOSITE: *The living room is a well-orchestrated interplay of diverse effects: a gilded Baroque console set into a mirrored alcove, the deep, rich tones of the walls and the curves of a Venetian glass chandelier.*

ABOVE: *Colorful patterned fabrics on ceiling, walls, table and chairs unify the Dining Room, with its collection of blue-and-white Chinese porcelains and Delft covered jars. Gladioli and irises echo the Oriental delicacy of an 18th-century Chinese lotus screen.*
RIGHT: *A dining table covered with brightly patterned linen and flanked by a pair of light Bertoia chairs sits in the peaceful Garden.*

*In the chintz-draped Bedroom, a Victorian
quilt and a contemporary painting by Dzubas
glow by the firelight. Paired 18th-century
Chinese lacquer chairs and sculptured geese
atop an ornate fireplace add dark accents.*

ABOVE: *Quilted wallcovering and patterned carpeting lend a cocoonlike feeling to the Bed/Sitting Room, accented by a vibrant bed-covering and bird-of-paradise flowers in a Chinese vase.* OPPOSITE: *A confettilike print adds a cozy air to a tiny Guest Room.*

PANACHE IN SMALL COMPASS

To recognize in the detritus and cast-off artifacts of urban life the raw stuff of an elegant and amenable interior demands a rather more venturesome stride of the imagination than many designers are prepared to take. Although main-line Modern Art discovered and exploited long ago the potential of "found objects" of industrial origin, interior design rarely sees their worth. It comes as a refreshing surprise to discover an interior such as New York designer Arthur Ferber has created in a quite standard city apartment. Here, industrial objects serve as furniture and also stand out as bold anchors in a design scheme of originality and polish.

The apartment was previously one of those unintriguing spaces often encountered in the highrise blocks that spring up among the many nineteenth-century loft buildings of Manhattan's now fashionable ex-manufacturing districts. "It was simply three boxes tied together, with nothing much to say for it," says Mr. Ferber. "But the apartment was in good condition, and the walls were clean. The building's architect had decided on bedroom, living room and the inevitable 'dining foyer'—a nauseating plan! Looking it over, I said to myself, 'Well, it certainly doesn't have to be this way.' "

Arthur Ferber feels that architects and designers frequently misunderstand the functional possibilities of rooms—particularly bedrooms. "Why not put pianos or dining room tables in them?" His own bedroom happily includes a desk-*cum*-dining table. "It has to be for special friends, but those are the only ones I have to sit-down dinners anyway. With larger groups I like to eat informally on the 'skid.' " The "skid" is exactly that: an industrial forklift skid used as a table in the living room, an eloquent indication of the interior designer's ability to recognize quality in seemingly useless objects.

He likes to call his apartment "a sophisticated version of the streets." There is much to be said for his definition. In addition to the skid table, two steel cylinders, abandoned at a construction site, were retrieved by the designer to serve as bases for end tables. Their mass, simplicity and sturdiness are both striking and tranquil. Restating his own reliance on basics in design, all the upholstered furniture is made from simple box shapes wrapped in quilted and glazed black chintz, providing a dynamic contrast to the metal street-found tables.

"But there is no *furniture* here in any conventional sense," says Mr. Ferber. And he goes on to explain that the primary forms of the upholstered pieces he designed give the interior a certain ease and flexibility. They state their functions simply, and they provide brilliant visual backgrounds for the dramatically punctuated "tablescapes" the designer delights in creating to vary the apartment's moods.

Arthur Ferber's interior, in many of its details, may have developed out of an industrial, or thoroughly urban, aesthetic—out of the impersonal and the collective. But it has the specific personality, or, as he describes it, "the certain strangeness" evident only in the finest and most individualistic contemporary residential design. "I'm really not an industrial designer, but a Minimal designer. Minimal can be elegant, though I don't think industrial can be."

Even given its fundamental originality and its bright flourishes of novelty, the tone of this interior is innovative rather than experimental, decisive rather than tentative. It is also polished, assured and mature in the elegance with which it is informed. The apartment, as Arthur Ferber describes it, is a place "where objects and people become very important, where they're appreciated and where the interior doesn't infringe upon them."

PRECEDING PAGE: *Designer Arthur Ferber's New York City apartment makes a dramatic Minimalist statement. A bright neon construction illuminates blocklike seating and industrial objects—including mirror-and-glass-topped steel pipe sections—that are used as furnishings.*

ABOVE AND RIGHT: *In the Bedroom, a laminated plastic table functions alternately as a desk and dining table. Lalique plates and Art Déco glasses highlight a table setting of light and dark contrasts. Steel and plexiglass folding chairs fit the starkness of the space.* OPPOSITE: *The upholstered bed floats in the center of the bedroom like a dark island. Floor-to-ceiling blinds and a linear painting by Jean-Marie Haessle repeat the vertical accents. On the quilted bedcovering, a mask on a lacquer tray adds a macabre Salome-like touch.*

IN THE TRADITIONAL GENRE

A warm, pervasive flow of light and strong color reflects and refracts across polished, glazed and mirrored surfaces, exposing multiple facets of extraordinarily refined furnishings and objects, contrasting with roughly woven Islamic rugs. The whole is reflected again in brilliantly lacquered ceilings. There is an audacious use of reds and blues and ochres that suggests a Spanish palace, a Baroque eclecticism and unwavering eye for true quality of surface, line, proportion. It's all there working together in Rubén de Saavedra's New York apartment.

"If I'd lived during the eighteenth century," he says, "I'd have been an architect and spent my time creating houses and furniture with a romantic involvement. It would have been pure joy for me." To be a designer, in his own mind, is the same as being an artist. The only difference is the format of the work. For him the field of interior design has fertile possibilities for becoming a vital part of daily life. "Designs grow better as people become more educated, travel, see and demand more of their environments," observes Mr. de Saavedra. "And I consider myself a creator. I know there are lots of clichés about not changing people's ways of life; not trying to influence them; not taking them into some milieu where they would be uncomfortable. But they do want me to help—to provide them with more and more elegance and sophistication."

Be that as it may, his style of work is most apparent in his own apartment. Each piece of his wide collection of ceramics, bronzes, terra-cottas, rugs and *objets de vertu* contributes its color and personality to the lively setting. He is an indefatigable collector of rare and glittering objects. And he also has the collector's curiosity. An unexpectedly lovely house noticed while traveling draws him irresistibly inside, to see whether there will be some added surprise, or some disappointment. Letdowns occur for him when a house seems right from the exterior but then reveals interior confusion created by owners who believe that exceptional structure and objects just naturally blend, without assistance.

"All experiences are important," says the designer. "Today, tomorrow and yesterday help you understand different ways of living. Then you evaluate what is best for yourself and do it." He constantly draws and finds his drawings an immediate and intimate exposure of a mind filled with the reflected schemes and fantasies of a true dreamer. He believes that a total effect is reached through unified effort, through knowing where one is starting from and through keeping one's eye on where one is going—not by pushing furniture around and letting things happen. "That's amateur hour," declares Rubén de Saavedra. "The eleventh commandment should be, 'Thou shalt have a decorator.'" Yet he never feels that his own taste or his particular way of life need be forced on his clients. He is as comfortable in creating an updated French or English interior as in producing some marvelous Chinese illusion. There are no restricting principles for him.

His aims are always clear, and he knows when they have been achieved. But he does not want his clients to feel that when a project is finished, his part in it is over. He wants them to know they can rely on him to make certain that everything stays perfect. Should they wish to elaborate a theme corresponding to their personal evolution, he is there to help. As often as not, his relationship to the project undergoes a regeneration beneficial to him and to his clients. He has the added pleasure of seeing them grow. "Not because of me," he says, "but because of themselves. Once they are introduced to new vistas, it often happens. They simply take off."

Designer Rubén de Saavedra's love of bold, dramatic color and his penchant for collecting rare objets d'art are vividly realized in his Manhattan apartment. PRECEDING PAGE: *Contemporary mirrors reflect a blend of traditional furnishings in the Living Room.*

The living room is a carefully orchestrated arrangement of contrasting styles. LEFT: *Dark lacquered walls are an effectively simple background for a delicate Régence gilt-framed looking glass, a pair of ornate Louis XV bronze and crystal sconces, and an 18th-century French portrait of a child. Matched metal-framed Directoire traveling mirrors repeat the geometric motif of the Moroccan rug.* OPPOSITE: *A grouping of rare objects and bibelots forms an appealing composition in a window corner. Jean-Pierre Cassigneul's* Lady at Deauville *gazes enigmatically over a bouquet of irises.*

RIGHT AND BELOW: *The richly formal Dining Room is the setting for more of Mr. de Saavedra's extensive collection: a bust by Pajou supported by a terra-cotta pedestal by Clodion, a painting by Bernard Klene and a group of porcelains housed in a Louis XVI secrétaire à l'anglaise. On the Louis XVI dining table, a tempting array of refreshments is enhanced by gold and silver flatware, a pair of gilt bronze Louis XVI candle-sticks and 1805 Sèvres plates.*

In the Master Bedroom, neutral tones temper the rich color of the canopy's bright cotton lining, the lacquered ceiling and the vivid hues of the bed pillows and chair upholstery. The Tunisian rug and the South Seas batik wallcovering over the bed add the vitality of pattern.

153

THE BLENDING OF STYLES

"I don't feel bound by any particular style or period," says antiques dealer Gene Tyson. "I'm not interested in being faithful to any one tradition, for tradition's sake." His home, a two-bedroom apartment twenty-two floors above one of Manhattan's most fashionable neighborhoods, is a clear demonstration of that philosophy. It brings together harmoniously such disparate elements as Egyptian artifacts, eighteenth-century French furniture, Thai sculpture and modern nonobjective art, all arranged to perfection in an appealing and graceful setting.

Mr. Tyson is fortunate in being able to combine his love of beautiful objects with his profession. His career as a dealer in fine antiques began quite by chance over twenty years ago in Philadelphia when his parents decided to divest themselves of a houseful of eighteenth-century French furniture and move to a smaller apartment. Since Philadelphia was then a poor market for French furniture, young Tyson volunteered to scout New York City. In the process, he met a number of established dealers, discovered that the business of buying and selling antiques was a fine art in itself, and set about his own education in all aspects of the French decorative arts. At that point he had a long way to go before achieving his present professionalism.

Recalling a visit he made, several years after he started his career, to the shop of a noted dealer in the town of Versailles, he smiles. "I had a friend with me who spoke good French," he relates, "and he and the owner began a lively conversation. I couldn't join in, so I took the liberty of poking around a little, assuming no one would notice. At one point I was down on my knees, with my head under a chair seat, when the owner looked my way. She thought this pretty odd behavior and asked my friend what in heaven's name I was doing! With him as translator, I replied that I was simply trying to tell if the chair were genuine." Mr. Tyson remembers feeling rather like one of Henry James's innocent Americans when she declared, "Tell him that if he cannot walk into a room and know by sight whether something is genuine, he will never be a dealer."

Though Gene Tyson eventually went into a far wider variety of antiques than eighteenth-century French (the growing scarcity of such pieces forces him to go as far afield as India, China and North Africa), he still takes special pride in the styles that launched him professionally. This can be seen in the effort he made to ensure that the chairs in his living room were upholstered perfectly. The three Régence armchairs were all sent to a master craftsman in Paris for the most exact re-covering. "It's awfully hard to settle for second best," says Mr. Tyson.

As a dealer, he is able to keep his personal collection as fluid as he chooses and to renew his surroundings regularly with recent acquisitions. Many of these will one day find their way to his shop, and ultimately to another, equally appreciative owner. Since the furniture changes with some regularity, perhaps the one constant in his apartment is pale color: a serene, unassertive beige tone. In satin-finished paint, the color wraps walls and ceilings throughout the apartment, and it covers the living room floor in the guise of a tightly woven carpet. The same tone covers the bedroom floors; even the fireplace conforms to his understated palette.

"Some people," he reflects, "find the low-key lighting and the relative lack of color a little strange. But you really can't be concerned too much by that sort of thing. I've done this place to please myself. There's plenty of space; the mood is always calm and restful; there are wonderful things to look at. I think you could call me a happy man here."

*Antiques dealer Gene Tyson
constantly changes and renews the
purposefully eclectic atmosphere
of his Manhattan apartment.*
PRECEDING PAGE: *Antique carved
ivory animals parade before a 19th-
century Thai figure and Lucite
sculptures by Jean-Claude Farhi.*

ABOVE: *A group of antiquities
on a Regency table includes a 600* B.C.
*Egyptian Osiris, a gilded Thai fan and
a Ming incense burner; a 17th-century
Syrian goat is stationed beneath.*
RIGHT: *The monochromatically toned
elements of the Living Room span
cultures and centuries.*

BELOW: *In the Living Room, an arresting oil painting by Felix Arauz offers sharp contrast to the sleek bronze deer—and its mirrored twin—by Elie Nadelman.*
OPPOSITE ABOVE: *Against a pale expanse of living room wall, a Lucite assemblage of silver brushes, by Arman, provides a bright focal point. Prowling carved animals add a whimsical and imaginative touch.*

LEFT: *An imposing Indian tiger, painted on cotton, stalks the width of the Bedroom wall. A graceful Louis XV caned side chair complements the molded curves of a silver lion from India. Standing solidly on the bedside table is a sturdy carved elephant.*

CREDITS

WRITERS

The following writers prepared the original *Architectural Digest* articles from which the material in this book has been adapted:

Mario Amaya

Peter Carlsen

David Halliday

Rosemary Kent

Valentine Lawford

John Loring

Wendy Murphy

David Rollins

Stephen Spector

All original text adapted by Sam Burchell.

Caption Writers:

Joanne Jaffe

Joyce Madison

Joyce Winkel

PHOTOGRAPHERS

Jaime Ardiles-Arce 16-23, 54-59, 92-97, 144-147

Richard Champion 24-31, 38-43, 78-85, 98-103, 110-119, 128-135, 136-143, 148-153

Michael Datoli 60-65

Angelo Donghia 104-109

Daniel Eifert 32-37

Feliciano 86-91

Horst 10-15, 120-127, 154-159

Norman McGrath 66-71

Peter Vitale 44-53, 72-77

DESIGN

Design Direction:

Philip Kaplan, Graphics Director

The Knapp Press

Book Design and Production:

Design Office/San Francisco

Bruce Kortebein

Cynthia Croker

Leigh McLellan